Weather Fun

by Allison K. Lim

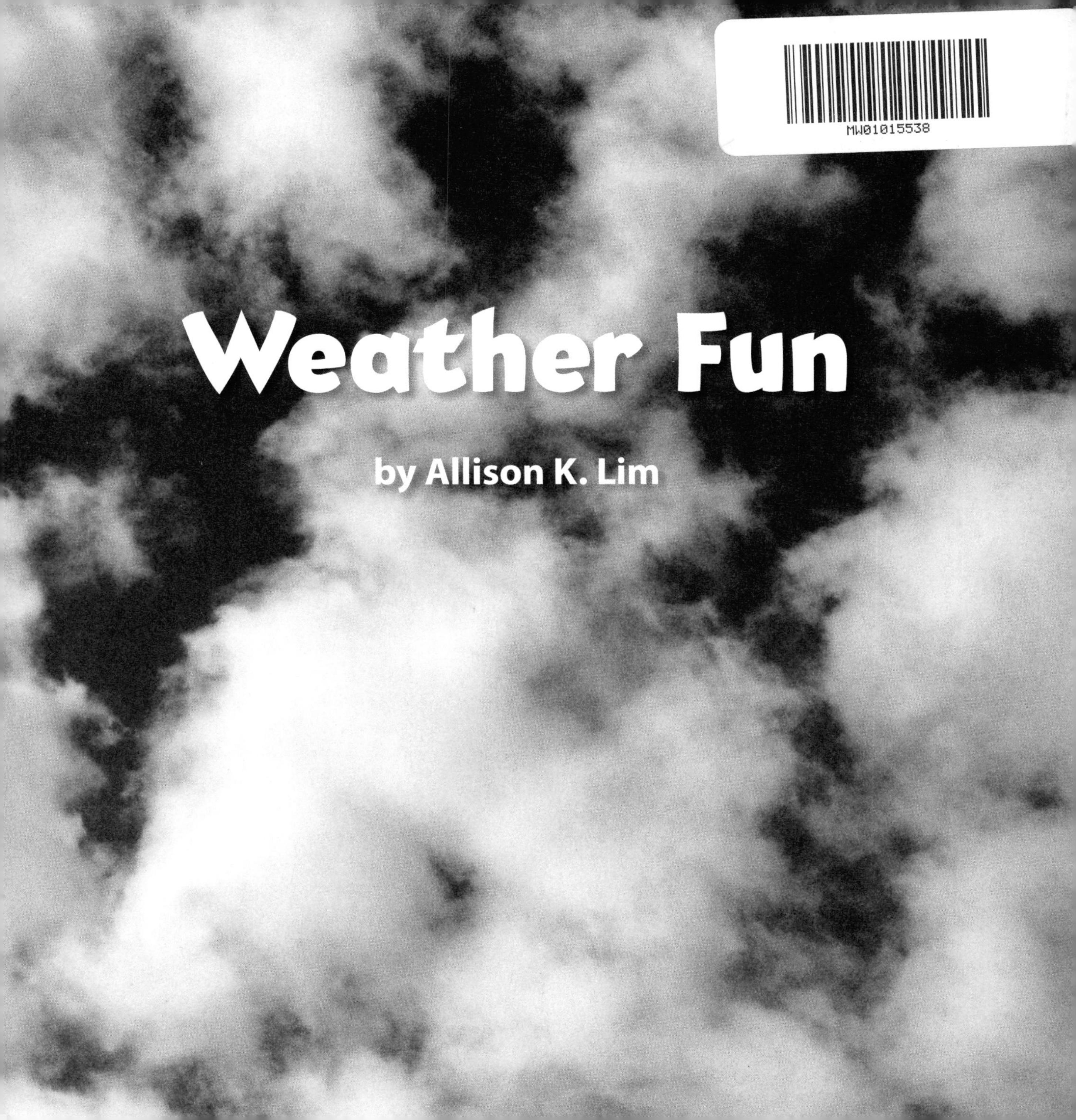

Sunny

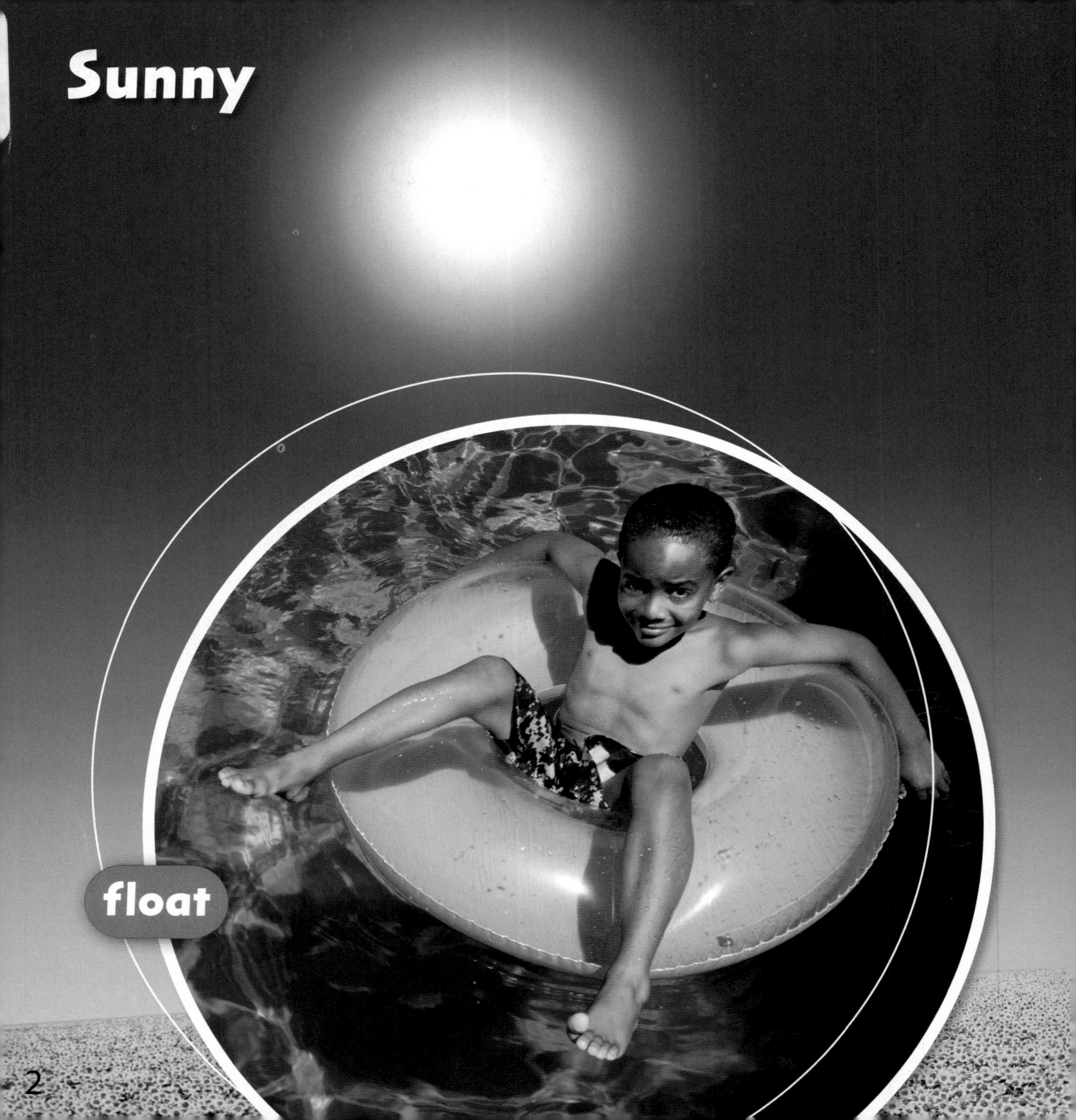

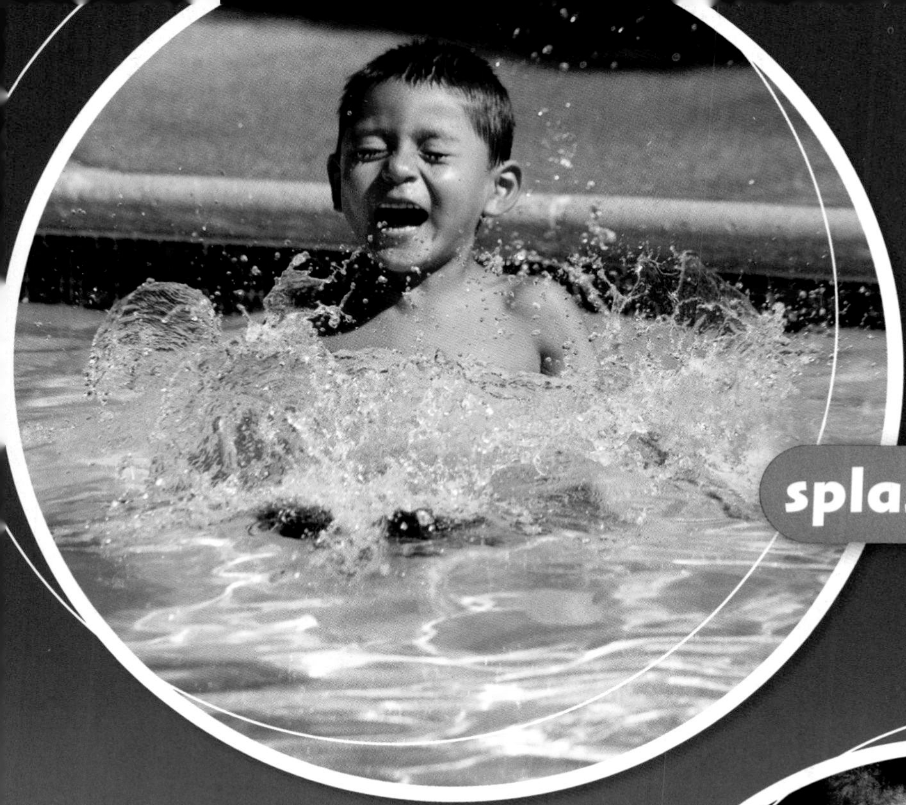

splash

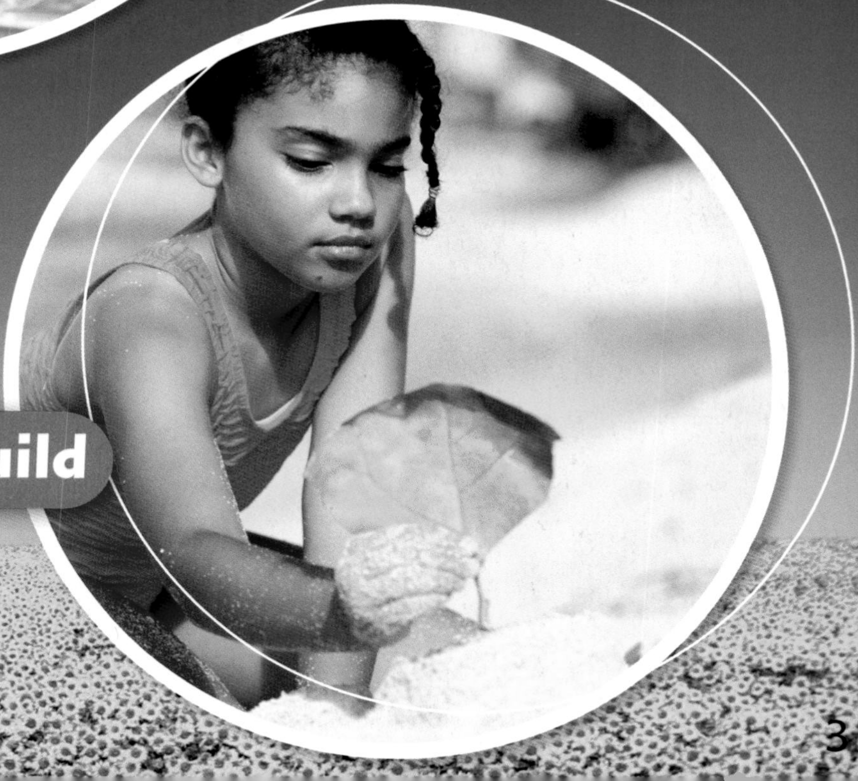

build

Cloudy

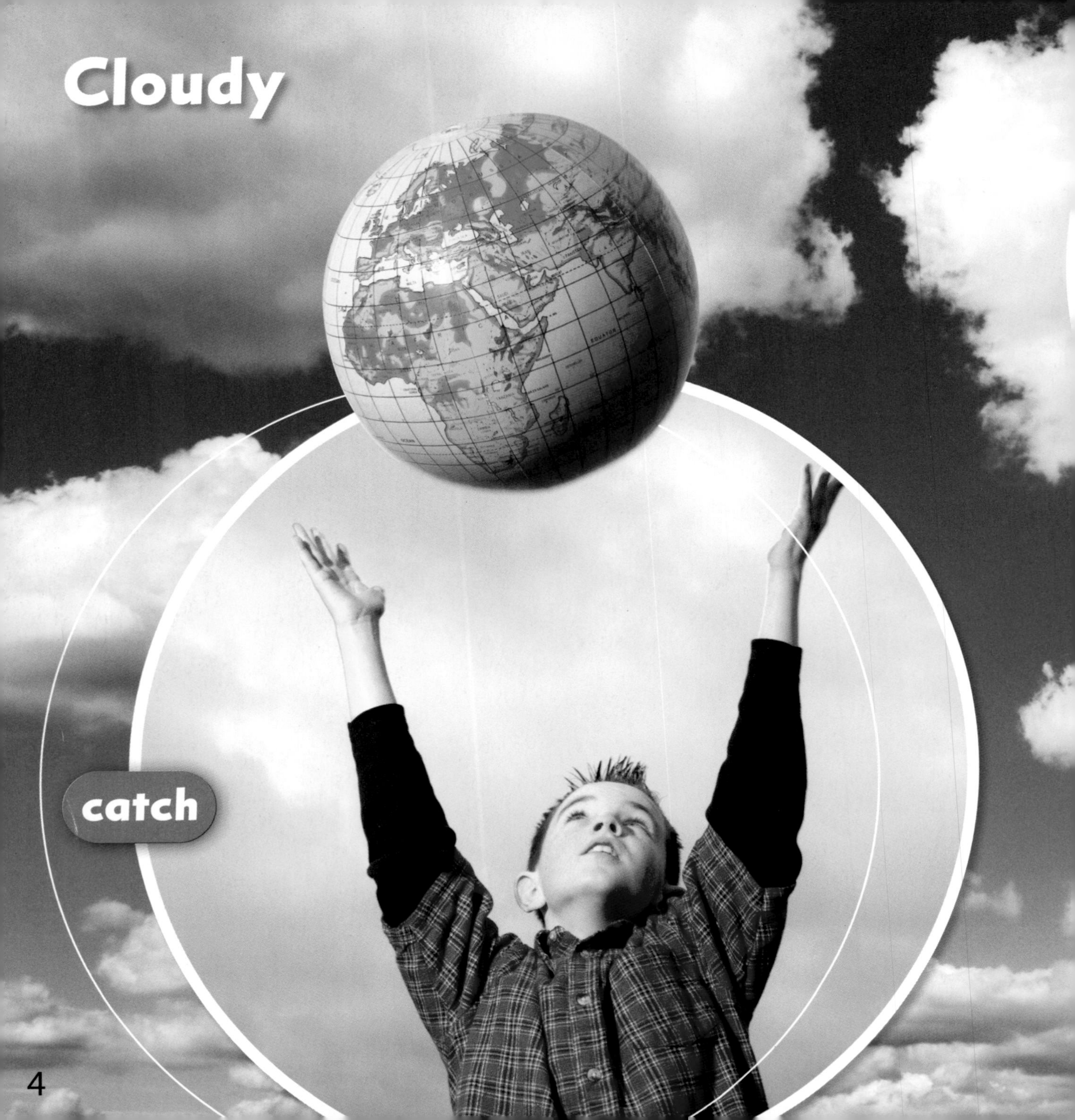

catch

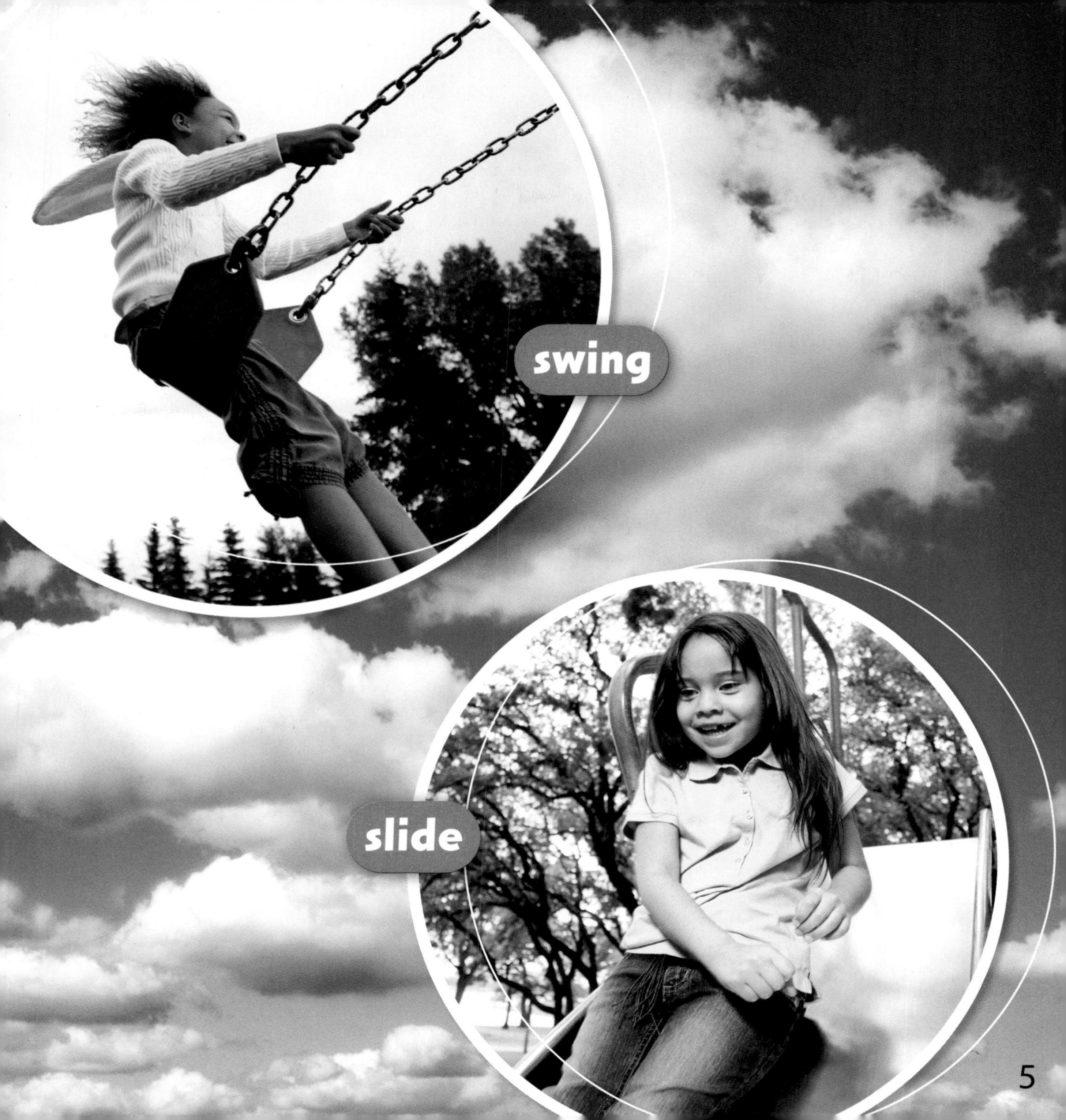
swing
slide

Snowy

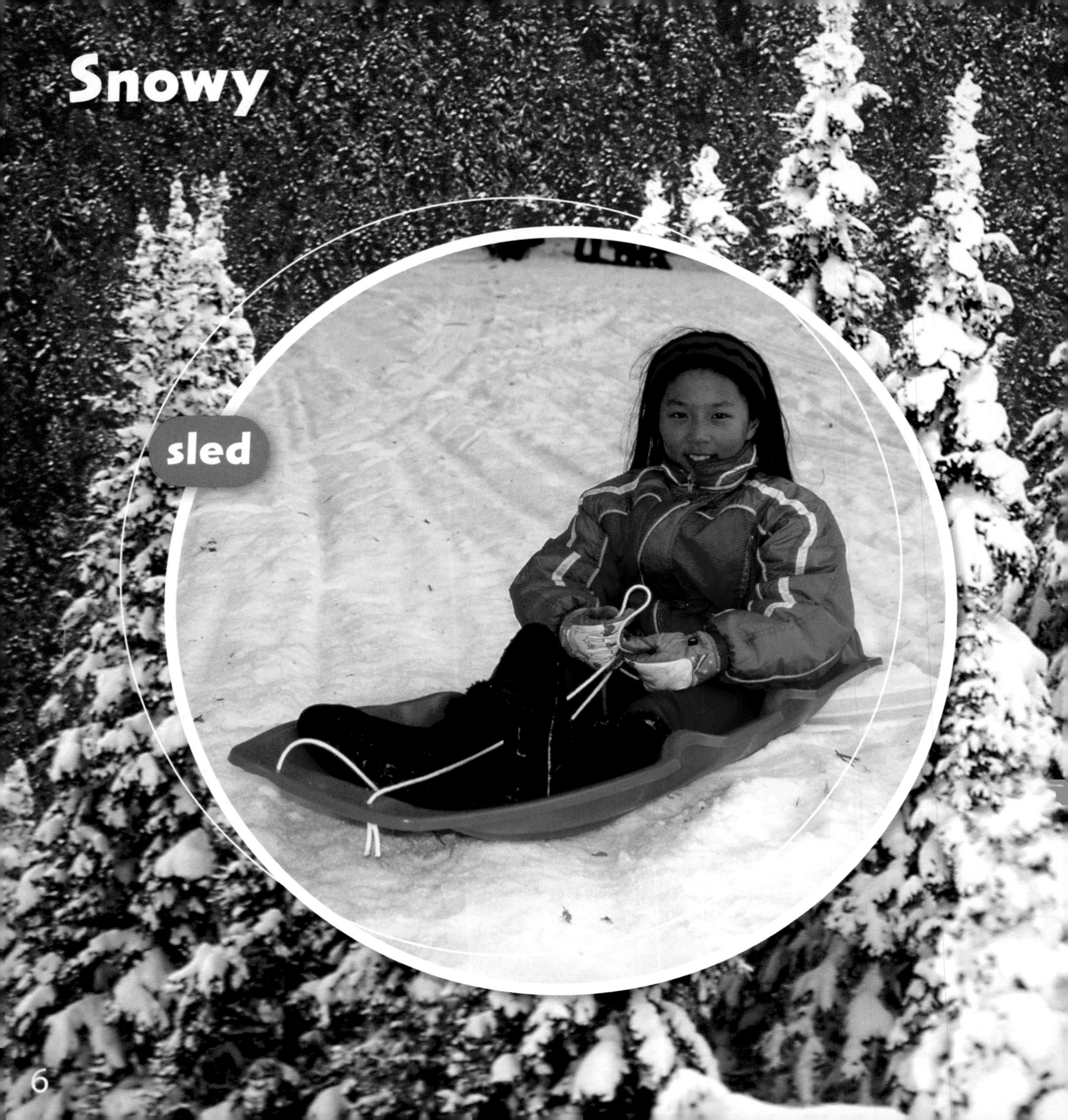

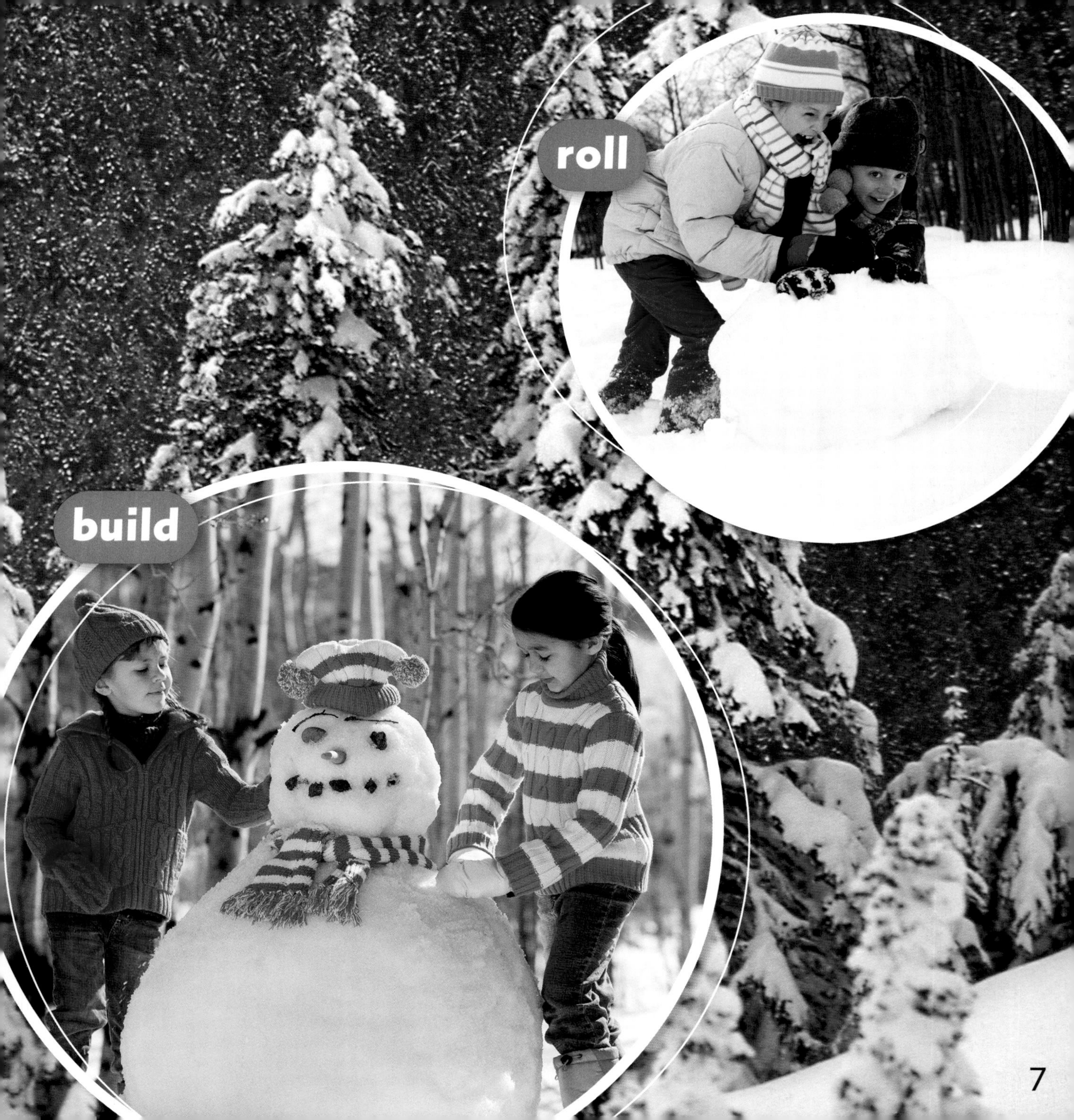
roll
build

Rainy

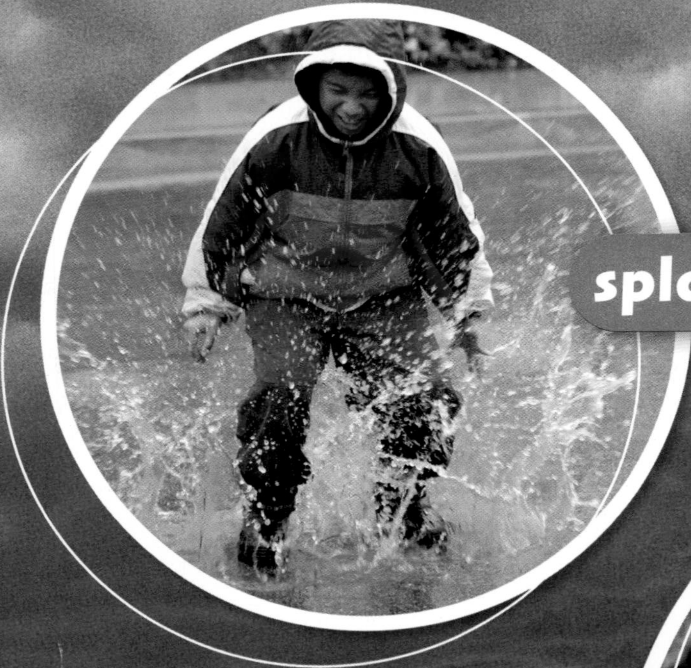

splash

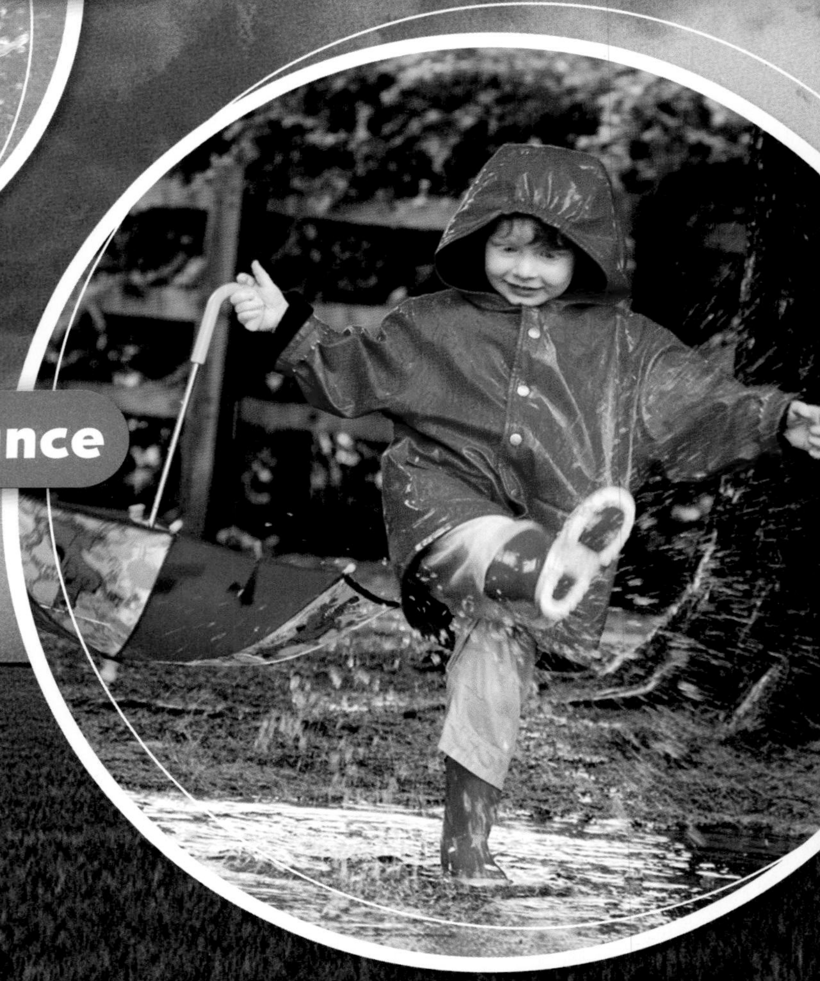

dance